SELF-MADE
Billionaire

In the US

GIRL,

Hold my beer!

First published by Aussie Trading LLC
Copyright © 2025 by Juan Rodulfo
All rights reserved.
No part of this publication may be reproduced, stored, or transmitted in any form or by any means, electronic, mechanical, photocopying, recording, scanning or otherwise without written permission from the publisher. It is illegal to copy this book, publish it on a website, or distribute it by any other means without permission.
Juan Rodulfo has no responsibility for the persistence or accuracy of URLs of external or third-party Internet websites referenced in this publication and does not warrant that the content of such websites is, or will remain, accurate or appropriate.
The names used by companies to distinguish their products are often claimed as trademarks. All trademarks and product names used in this book and on its cover, trade names, service marks, trademarks are trademarks of their respective owners. The publishers and the book are not associated with any products or suppliers mentioned in this book. None of the companies or organizations referenced in the book have endorsed it.
Library of Congress Catalog
Names: Rodulfo, Juan
ISBN: 979-8-3493-7555-2 (e-book)
ISBN: 979-8-3494-0584-6 (paperback)
ISBN: 979-8-3494-0585-3 (hardcover)
First edition
Layout by Juan Rodulfo
Cover art by Guaripete Solutions
Production: Aussie Trading, LLC
books@aussietrading.ltd
Printed in the USA

"Oh America, how often have you taken necessities from the masses to give luxuries to the classes...God never intended for one group of people to live in superfluous inordinate wealth, while others live in abject deadening poverty."
**Dr. Martin Luther King, Jr. *(1929-1968)*
American civil rights leader, November 4, 1956**

Preface

The American Dream promises that hard work and ingenuity lead to success. Yet, behind the glimmering facade of "self-made" billionaires lies a rigged system, meticulously designed to funnel wealth and power to a privileged few. This book, "SELF-MADE BILLIONAIRE in the US, GIRL, hold my beer!", dismantles the myth of meritocracy, exposing how billionaires amass fortunes not through grit alone, but through systemic exploitation, taxpayer-funded handouts, and legalized greed.

The Myth vs. The Machine

The notion that billionaires like Elon Musk or Jeff Bezos are lone geniuses who "pulled themselves up by their bootstraps" is a seductive lie. In reality, their wealth is built on pillars of privilege: tax codes rigged in their favor, corporate welfare, and labor practices straight out of the Gilded Age. Consider this: while the average worker pays a higher tax rate than billionaires (Chapter 1), Elon Musk's empire has siphoned $38 billion in public subsidies (Chapter 2). Meanwhile, Amazon and Walmart crush unions (Chapter 3), and Silicon Valley titans lobby for policies that turn every $1 of political spending into $130 of tax breaks (Chapter 4). This isn't capitalism—it's kleptocracy.

Exploitation Without Borders

The exploitation isn't confined to U.S. soil. Apple and Nike hoard $245 billion offshore (Chapter 5), while Tesla's cobalt mines in Congo and Walmart's sweatshops in Bangladesh reveal a global race to the bottom. Billionaires don't "create wealth"; they extract it—from workers, communities, and the planet (Chapter 5). Even the myth of meritocracy crumbles under scrutiny: 70% of the Forbes 400 inherited wealth or grew up affluent (Chapter 6). Steve Jobs, adopted by a machinist, is the exception; Elon Musk, heir to an emerald fortune, is the rule.

The Human Cost

This system isn't just unequal—it's violent. Amazon warehouses in Black neighborhoods have 50% higher injury rates (Chapter 7). Prison laborers earn $0.20/hour building tech infrastructure (Chapter 7). Women, comprising 70% of Walmart's workforce, are denied living wages (Chapter 7). Even philanthropy becomes a tool for evasion: Bezos' $100M donation to Dolly Parton costs him $0 in taxes, while Amazon fights a $2B IRS bill (Chapter 8).

A Path Forward

But this book isn't just an indictment—it's a blueprint for change. Chapter 9 demands we tax unrealized gains, mandate worker ownership, and redirect subsidies to housing, healthcare, and renewables. The goal? Not to shame individuals, but to dismantle a system that equates wealth with worth.

Why This Book Matters

In an era of spiraling inequality, "SELF-MADE BILLIONAIRE in the US, GIRL, hold my beer!" is a call to action. It strips away the fairy tales of "job creators" and "trickle-down economics," revealing a reality where billionaires profit from our labor, our data, and our democracy. The solutions are within reach—if we dare to reimagine equity.

Buckle up. The truth isn't just stranger than fiction—it's more outrageous.

Juan Rodulfo
June 2025

"A searing exposé that replaces bootstrap mythology with cold, hard facts—and a roadmap for revolution."

— For further insights, visit juanrodulfo.com.

The Tax Code Loophole Playbook: How Billionaires Pay Less Than You

The American tax system is widely believed to be progressive, designed so that those with the greatest means shoulder the largest share of the nation's tax burden. But for the ultra-wealthy, this principle is more myth than reality. While working Americans pay taxes on every paycheck, billionaires exploit legal loopholes to reduce their effective tax rates to as little as 1%—far below the rates paid by median workers (ProPublica, 2021[i]; ITEP, 2023[ii]). This article examines the strategies that enable this disparity, the billionaires who use them, and the policy failures that perpetuate legalized wealth hoarding.

1. Wealth vs. Income: The Legal Distinction

At the heart of the billionaire tax advantage is the fundamental distinction between income and wealth. Under U.S. law, income—wages, salaries, and bonuses—is taxed as it is earned. But wealth—especially in the form of unrealized capital gains from stocks, real estate, and other appreciating assets—is taxed only when those assets are sold (ProPublica, 2021; SmartAsset, 2025[iii]).

For most Americans, income is the primary source of tax liability. For billionaires, however, the bulk of their net worth is tied up in assets that grow in value year after year, but which are not taxed until sold. This means that while their net worth soars, their taxable income—and thus their tax bill—remains negligible (ProPublica, 2021; ITEP, 2023).

2. The Buy-Borrow-Die Strategy

The "buy-borrow-die" strategy is the cornerstone of billionaire tax avoidance. It consists of three simple steps:

Buy

Billionaires accumulate vast portfolios of stocks, real estate, and other appreciating assets. These investments grow in value, but because the gains are unrealized, they are not taxed (SmartAsset, 2025; PBS, 2025[iv]).

Borrow

When billionaires need cash, they borrow against their assets rather than selling them. Banks are eager to lend to the ultra-wealthy, offering low interest rates and large credit lines. The interest on these loans is often tax-deductible, and the loan proceeds are not considered income, so no tax is owed (SmartAsset, 2025; PBS, 2025).

For example, Larry Ellison, co-founder of Oracle, secured a $10 billion credit line using his shares as collateral, allowing him to fund major purchases—including a $300 million Hawaiian island—without triggering capital gains taxes (SmartAsset, 2025; PBS, 2025).

Die

When billionaires die, their heirs inherit the assets at their current market value, resetting the cost basis. This "stepped-up basis" erases all past capital gains, allowing heirs to sell the assets immediately without paying any capital gains tax (SmartAsset, 2025; PBS, 2025).

3. Case Studies: Elon Musk and Larry Ellison

Elon Musk

Elon Musk, CEO of Tesla and SpaceX, has perfected the art of tax avoidance. He takes no salary from his companies, instead receiving stock options and awards. When he needs cash, he borrows against his Tesla shares, accessing billions tax-free. In 2021, Musk paid an effective tax rate of just 0.3% on a $140 billion increase in net worth (ProPublica, 2021; SmartAsset, 2025).

Musk's approach is emblematic of the buy-borrow-die strategy. By never selling his shares, he avoids capital gains taxes. Instead, he uses his vast wealth as collateral for loans, accessing cash without triggering a taxable event.

Larry Ellison

Larry Ellison, founder of Oracle, has used his shares as collateral for personal loans, including a $10 billion credit line. This allows him to fund lavish purchases without selling shares or triggering taxes. Ellison's strategy is a textbook example of the buy-borrow-die playbook (SmartAsset, 2025; PBS, 2025).

4. Other Tax Avoidance Tactics

Real Estate and Depreciation

Billionaires invest heavily in real estate, taking advantage of depreciation deductions and mortgage interest write-offs. They can also borrow against their properties, accessing cash without selling (SmartAsset, 2025).

Charitable Donations and Foundations

Philanthropy is another popular tax avoidance tool. Billionaires can donate to their own foundations, claim immediate tax deductions, and decide later how to distribute the money (SmartAsset, 2025; PBS, 2025).

Business Expenses

By converting personal assets—such as yachts, jets, and vacation homes—into business assets, billionaires can deduct maintenance, fuel, and staff costs as business expenses (SmartAsset, 2025; PBS, 2025).

5. Policy Failure: Decades of Tax Cuts and IRS Defunding

The Shift Toward Inequality

Since the 1980s, tax policy in the U.S. has increasingly favored the wealthy. Top marginal tax rates have been slashed, capital gains taxes reduced, and estate taxes weakened (ITEP, 2023; CNBC, 2025). The result is a system where the richest Americans pay a lower effective tax rate than many middle-class families (ProPublica, 2021).

Defunding the IRS

The IRS has been systematically defunded over the past decade, reducing its ability to audit the wealthy. Between 2010 and 2020, the IRS lost 33% of its enforcement staff, and audits of millionaires fell by 80% (ProPublica, 2021; ITEP, 2023). This has made it easier for billionaires to exploit loopholes without fear of scrutiny.

The Medicare Tax Loophole

Even when new taxes are introduced to target the wealthy, loopholes remain. For example, the Net Investment Income Tax (NIIT) was intended to capture investment income, but business owners can exempt gains from the sale of their businesses. In the first six years of the law, 17 individuals shielded at least $1 billion each from tax, saving a combined $1.3 billion (ProPublica, 2024[v]).

6. The Human Cost: Inequality and the Middle Class

The Growing Wealth Gap

The tax code's favoritism toward the wealthy has contributed to historic levels of inequality. The top 1% now controls more wealth than the bottom 90% combined (ITEP, 2023). Meanwhile, middle-class families struggle with stagnant wages and rising costs.

The Burden on Working Americans

While billionaires pay effective tax rates as low as 1%, the median American worker pays 13–14% on their income (ITEP, 2023). This disparity undermines faith in the tax system and fuels political polarization.

7. Reform Proposals and Political Resistance

Closing the Loopholes

Advocates for tax reform have proposed a range of solutions, including taxing unrealized capital gains, eliminating the stepped-up basis, and increasing IRS enforcement (ProPublica, 2021; ITEP, 2023; Senator Warren, 2024[vi]).

Political Obstacles

Despite widespread public support for closing tax loopholes, political resistance from wealthy donors and corporate interests has stymied reform efforts (CNBC, 2025; Senator

Warren, 2024). Recent tax bills, such as the House Republican "big beautiful" tax bill, have further favored the rich (CNBC, 2025[vii]).

8. International Comparisons

Lessons from Abroad

Other developed countries have taken steps to close tax loopholes and ensure that the wealthy pay their fair share. For example, many European nations have higher capital gains taxes and stricter enforcement mechanisms (ITEP, 2023).

The Global Race to the Bottom

However, the global nature of wealth means that billionaires can often shift assets to low-tax jurisdictions, making international cooperation essential for effective reform (ITEP, 2023).

Welfare for the Wealthy: The $38 Billion Government Handout

In the American imagination, welfare is often associated with social safety nets for the poor. Yet, the most generous welfare system in the United States is not for the indigent, but for the ultra-wealthy. Over the past two decades, billionaires like Elon Musk and Jeff Bezos have amassed fortunes not just through innovation and hard work, but through massive government handouts—grants, tax credits, and lucrative contracts—totaling tens of billions of dollars, all funded by taxpayers (Washington Post, 2025[viii]; Good Jobs First, 2025[ix]; Fortune, 2025[x]). This article explores the myth of the "self-made" billionaire, the rise of corporate socialism, and the consequences of privatizing gains while socializing losses.

1. Subsidy Kings: Elon Musk's $38 Billion Empire

The Scale of the Handout

Elon Musk, the world's richest person, is often celebrated as a visionary entrepreneur. What is less discussed is how much of his success has been underwritten by public funds. According to a Washington Post investigation,

Musk and his companies—Tesla, SpaceX, and others—have received at least $38 billion in government contracts, loans, subsidies, and tax credits since 2003 (Washington Post, 2025; Good Jobs First, 2025; Lemonde, 2025[xi]). This figure is likely an undercount, as it does not include classified defense and intelligence contracts, which are not publicly disclosed (Good Jobs First, 2025; NPR, 2025[xii]).

The Breakdown

- Tesla: Nearly $16 billion in aid, including tax credits, grants, and the sale of carbon credits to other automakers. The federal government's $7,500 tax credit for electric vehicle buyers has also boosted Tesla's sales (Lemonde, 2025; Washington Post, 2025).
- SpaceX: Around $22.6 billion in government contracts, primarily from NASA and the Pentagon. SpaceX has become the preferred supplier for both civilian and military space missions, including the International Space Station and classified spy satellite launches (Lemonde, 2025; Wired, 2025[xiii]).
- State and Local Support: At least $1.5 billion in tax credits, grants, and reimbursements from eight states, with an additional $2.1 billion from various government agencies (Good Jobs First, 2025; Washington Post, 2025).

The Timing

Nearly two-thirds of this $38 billion windfall was allocated in the last five years, with 2024 alone seeing at least $6.3 billion in new commitments—a record high (Washington Post, 2025; Lemonde, 2025). This surge coincides with increased federal support for electric vehicles and space exploration, sectors where Musk's companies are market leaders.

2. The Mechanics of Corporate Welfare

Grants, Tax Credits, and Contracts

Musk's companies have benefited from a variety of government mechanisms:
- Direct Grants and Loans: Tesla received a $465 million loan from the Department of Energy in 2010, which was repaid with interest but provided critical liquidity during a near-bankruptcy crisis (Lemonde, 2025).
- Tax Credits: Tesla and its customers have benefited from federal and state tax credits for electric vehicles and renewable energy (Washington Post, 2025; Lemonde, 2025).
- Government Contracts: SpaceX's contracts with NASA and the Pentagon are the backbone of its revenue, with billions allocated

for launches, cargo missions, and classified projects (Wired, 2025; Washington Post, 2025).

The Subsidy Harvesting Strategy

Musk's "subsidy harvesting strategy" is not unique to him, but it is executed on an unprecedented scale. His companies have positioned themselves to capture every available government incentive, from electric vehicle credits to space exploration contracts (Fortune, 2025). This strategy has allowed Musk to build a business empire that is as much a product of public policy as private enterprise.

3. Corporate Socialism: Amazon's HQ2 and State-Funded Stadiums

The HQ2 Extortion Racket

Amazon's search for a second headquarters (HQ2) in 2017–2018 was a masterclass in corporate welfare. The company solicited bids from cities across North America, pitting them against each other in a race to offer the most generous tax breaks and incentives. The eventual winners—New York City and Northern Virginia—promised billions in tax credits, infrastructure investments, and other perks (New York Times, 2018; Brookings, 2019).

When public backlash forced Amazon to withdraw from New York, the company still secured a $750 million incentive package in Virginia. This "extortion racket" demonstrated how multinational corporations can leverage their economic power to extract public funds, often at the expense of local services and infrastructure (Brookings, 2019[xiv]; New York Times, 2018[xv]).

State-Funded Stadiums

The phenomenon is not limited to tech giants. Professional sports teams routinely demand—and receive—hundreds of millions in public subsidies for new stadiums. These deals are justified as economic development, but studies show they rarely deliver promised benefits. Instead, they funnel taxpayer dollars into the pockets of billionaire owners (Brookings, 2016[xvi]; The Atlantic, 2015).

4. Privatized Gains, Socialized Losses: COVID Bailouts

The Great Bailout

The COVID-19 pandemic exposed the stark reality of America's economic system: when times are good, profits are privatized; when times are bad, losses are socialized. The federal government authorized trillions in relief funds, much of which went to large corporations and financial institutions (ProPublica, 2020[xvii]; The Guardian, 2020).

- Corporate Bailouts: Companies like Boeing, Carnival Cruise Lines, and major airlines received billions in loans and grants, even as they laid off workers and paid out dividends to shareholders (ProPublica, 2020; The Guardian, 2020[xviii]).

- Stock Buybacks: Many companies used bailout funds to prop up their stock prices through buybacks, enriching executives and investors while workers faced unemployment and pay cuts (ProPublica, 2020; The Guardian, 2020).

- Worker Layoffs: Despite receiving public funds, some of the largest recipients laid off thousands of employees, underscoring the disconnect between corporate welfare and worker welfare (ProPublica, 2020; The Guardian, 2020).

5. The Consequences of Welfare for the Wealthy

Erosion of Public Trust

The perception that the system is rigged in favor of the rich undermines public trust in government and democracy. When billionaires receive billions in subsidies while ordinary Americans struggle to make ends meet, it fuels cynicism and political polarization (Brookings, 2019; The Atlantic, 2015).

Widening Inequality

Corporate welfare exacerbates economic inequality by concentrating wealth and power in the hands of a few. The $38 billion in subsidies to Musk's companies, the billions extracted by Amazon, and the trillions in COVID bailouts all contribute to a system where the rich get richer at the expense of the public (Washington Post, 2025; ProPublica, 2020).

Missed Opportunities

Every dollar spent on corporate welfare is a dollar not spent on education, healthcare, infrastructure, or other public goods. The opportunity cost of these subsidies is immense, and the benefits are often overstated (Brookings, 2019; The Atlantic, 2015[xix]).

6. The Political Economy of Corporate Welfare

The Role of Lobbying

The ability of companies like Tesla, SpaceX, and Amazon to secure such massive subsidies is not just a function of their economic importance, but also their political influence. These companies spend millions on lobbying, campaign contributions, and public relations to shape policy in their favor (OpenSecrets, 2023; Fortune, 2025).

The Myth of the Free Market

The rhetoric of free markets and limited government obscures the reality of corporate socialism. In practice, the state plays a central role in subsidizing and protecting the interests of large corporations, often at the expense of smaller businesses and the public (Brookings, 2019; The Atlantic, 2015).

7. Case Studies: Musk vs. Bezos

Musk's Subsidy Harvesting

Elon Musk's companies have become synonymous with government support. From Tesla's electric vehicle credits to SpaceX's NASA contracts, Musk has built an empire on public funds (Washington Post, 2025; Good Jobs First, 2025; Fortune, 2025).

Bezos's Amazon Empire

Jeff Bezos, founder of Amazon, has also benefited from billions in tax breaks, infrastructure subsidies, and COVID relief. Amazon's HQ2 saga and its dominance in e-commerce are testaments to the power of corporate welfare (New York Times, 2018; Brookings, 2019).

8. The Way Forward: Reforming Corporate Welfare

Transparency and Accountability

Greater transparency in government contracts and subsidies is essential to hold companies accountable. Public databases like Good Jobs First's Subsidy Tracker have shed light on the scale of corporate welfare, but more needs to be done (Good Jobs First, 2025; Washington Post, 2025).

Ending the Extortion Racket

Cities and states should refuse to participate in bidding wars for corporate headquarters and stadiums. Instead, they should invest in public goods that benefit all residents, not just billionaire owners (Brookings, 2019; The Atlantic, 2015).

Prioritizing Public Goods

Public funds should be directed toward education, healthcare, infrastructure, and other services that promote broad-based prosperity, not narrow corporate interests (Brookings, 2019; The Atlantic, 2015).

The $38 billion government handout to Elon Musk's empire, the billions extracted by Amazon, and the trillions in COVID bailouts are not anomalies—they are features of a system that prioritizes the interests of the wealthy over those of ordinary Americans. Corporate socialism is alive and well in the United States, and it is time to demand an end to welfare for the wealthy.

Union Busting 101: Crushing Worker Power to Maximize Profits

The American labor movement, once a powerful force for worker rights, now faces a relentless and sophisticated corporate counteroffensive. Companies like Amazon, Starbucks, and Walmart have developed extensive anti-union toolkits to suppress organizing, maintain low wages, and maximize profits. These tactics—ranging from surveillance and captive-audience meetings to retaliatory firings and propaganda—are designed to crush worker power and deter collective action. This article examines the methods, impacts, and consequences of union busting in three of America's largest corporations.

1. The Anatomy of Union Busting

Union busting is not a new phenomenon, but its methods have grown increasingly sophisticated. Today's corporations employ a mix of legal and illegal tactics to undermine organizing efforts, from psychological manipulation to outright coercion. The goal is clear: prevent workers from forming unions, maintain managerial control, and keep labor costs low (EPI, 2025[xx]; The Nation, 2025[xxi]).

2. Amazon's Anti-Union Toolkit

Surveillance and Intimidation

At Amazon fulfillment centers, union organizers describe an environment of fear and intimidation. Managers and HR professionals are flown in from across the country to patrol the shop floor, monitor worker conversations, and identify potential union supporters (The Nation, 2025; LaborLab, 2025[xxii]). Surveillance is both overt and covert: security cameras are ubiquitous, and workers report being watched during breaks and on the warehouse floor.

Captive-Audience Meetings

Amazon holds mandatory "captive-audience" meetings, where workers are required to listen to anti-union presentations. These meetings are led by managers or outside consultants, who deliver scripted messages warning that unions will take away benefits, limit flexibility, and deduct dues from paychecks (The Nation, 2025; EPI, 2025). Workers are often shown anti-union videos on loops in break rooms, and managers repeat talking points in small group settings.

Retaliatory Firings and Discipline

Retaliation is a cornerstone of Amazon's anti-union strategy. Organizers and union supporters are targeted with disciplinary actions, reduced hours, or outright termination (EPI, 2025; The Nation, 2025). At the RDU1 warehouse in North Carolina, for example, workers reported that managers threatened to fire anyone caught discussing unionization. In some cases, managers have spread false rumors about union organizers, including claims that supporting a union could lead to deportation (The Nation, 2025; LaborLab, 2025).

Propaganda and Division

Amazon bombards workers with anti-union messages through company apps, text alerts, and posters. The company also exploits racial and ethnic divisions, using fear tactics to discourage solidarity among workers of color (The Nation, 2025; LaborLab, 2025). At the Garner warehouse, managers reportedly told Black and Hispanic workers that unionization could threaten their jobs or immigration status.

Legal and Financial Firepower

Amazon spends tens of millions of dollars on anti-union consultants and law firms. In 2022 alone, the company paid over $14 million to outside consultants, who are dispatched to warehouses whenever organizing efforts emerge (EPI, 2025). Amazon also employs an army of internal "employee relations experts" to monitor and suppress worker activism.

3. Starbucks' Union Avoidance

Closing Unionized Stores

Starbucks has responded to unionization efforts by closing stores that have voted to unionize. In several cases, the company has shuttered locations shortly after workers won union elections, sending a clear message to employees at other stores (EPI, 2025; EPI Press, 2025[xxiii]). These closures are often justified as "business decisions," but workers and labor advocates see them as retaliation.

Denying Benefits to Pro-Union Workers

Starbucks has also denied wage increases and benefit improvements to workers at unionized stores, while offering them to nonunion employees (EPI, 2025; EPI Press, 2025). This two-tier system is designed to discourage unionization by making it seem like a disadvantage.

Stalling Negotiations

Even when workers succeed in forming a union, Starbucks has used stalling tactics to delay contract negotiations. The company has refused to bargain in good faith, dragging out the process and leaving workers without the benefits of collective bargaining (EPI, 2025; EPI Press, 2025).

4. Walmart's Wage Suppression

Poverty Wages

Walmart is notorious for paying poverty wages, particularly to its front-line workers. Many employees rely on public assistance to make ends meet, despite the company's record profits (EPI, 2025). Walmart's business model depends on keeping labor costs as low as possible, which means suppressing wages and benefits.

Anti-Union Propaganda

Walmart has a long history of anti-union activity. The company trains managers to identify and suppress organizing efforts, and it has closed stores where workers have attempted to unionize (EPI, 2025). Walmart also uses propaganda to convince workers that unions are unnecessary or harmful, often citing the risk of lost jobs or reduced flexibility.

High Turnover and Worker Disempowerment

By keeping wages low and turnover high, Walmart ensures that workers are less likely to organize. The company's anti-union toolkit includes strict scheduling policies, limited benefits, and a culture of fear and intimidation (EPI, 2025). Workers who speak out or attempt to organize are often disciplined or fired.

5. The Legal Landscape

Weak Labor Laws

U.S. labor laws are notoriously weak when it comes to protecting workers' right to organize. Employers face few meaningful penalties for violating labor laws, and the enforcement process is slow and cumbersome

(EPI, 2025; LaborLab, 2025). As a result, companies like Amazon, Starbucks, and Walmart can engage in union busting with relative impunity.

NLRB Challenges

The National Labor Relations Board (NLRB) is responsible for enforcing labor laws, but its effectiveness has been undermined by political interference and underfunding (LaborLab, 2025). During the Trump administration, for example, the NLRB was left without a functioning board, rendering it unable to issue decisions on labor disputes (LaborLab, 2025).

Unfair Labor Practices

Despite these challenges, workers have filed hundreds of unfair labor practice charges against Amazon, Starbucks, and Walmart. As of January 2025, the NLRB had over 350 open or settled cases against Amazon alone (EPI, 2025). These cases include allegations of retaliatory firings, threats, and other illegal tactics.

6. The Human Cost

Fear and Intimidation

Union busting creates a climate of fear and intimidation in the workplace. Workers who attempt to organize risk losing their jobs, facing disciplinary action, or being ostracized by management (The Nation, 2025; LaborLab, 2025). This atmosphere discourages collective action and leaves workers feeling powerless.

Economic Insecurity

By suppressing wages and benefits, union busting perpetuates economic insecurity for millions of workers. Many employees at Amazon, Starbucks, and Walmart struggle to make ends meet, despite working full-time (EPI, 2025). The lack of union representation means that workers have little bargaining power to improve their conditions.

Social Division

Union busting also exploits social divisions, pitting workers against each other along racial, ethnic, or ideological lines (The Nation, 2025; LaborLab, 2025). Companies like Amazon have been accused of using fear tactics to discourage solidarity among workers of color, further fragmenting the workforce.

7. The Broader Implications

Erosion of Worker Rights

The rise of corporate union busting represents a broader erosion of worker rights in the United States. As companies grow more aggressive in their anti-union campaigns, workers are left with fewer protections and less power to advocate for themselves (EPI, 2025; LaborLab, 2025).

Impact on Democracy

Union busting also undermines democracy by concentrating power in the hands of corporate executives and shareholders. When workers are unable to organize, they have little say in the decisions that affect their lives and livelihoods (EPI, 2025).

Global Reach

The tactics used by Amazon, Starbucks, and Walmart are not limited to the United States. These companies have exported their anti-union strategies to other countries, where they face similar accusations of labor rights violations (Foxglove, 2025[xxiv]; UNI Global Union, 2025[xxv]).

8. Resistance and Hope

Despite the odds, workers continue to organize and fight for their rights. At Amazon's RDU1 warehouse, for example, workers formed the Carolina Amazonians United for Solidarity and Empowerment (CAUSE) and mounted a spirited organizing campaign (The Nation, 2025; LaborLab, 2025). Although the effort was ultimately crushed by Amazon's anti-union machine, it inspired workers at other facilities to keep fighting.

Similarly, Starbucks workers have formed the Starbucks Workers United union, which has won recognition at hundreds of stores across the country (EPI, 2025). These victories, though hard-won, demonstrate that worker solidarity can overcome even the most sophisticated union-busting tactics.

Union busting is a deliberate and systematic strategy to crush worker power and maximize corporate profits. Companies like Amazon, Starbucks, and Walmart have developed extensive toolkits to suppress organizing, maintain low wages, and keep workers divided. These tactics—ranging from surveillance and captive-audience meetings to retaliatory firings and propaganda—are designed to intimidate and disempower workers.

Billionaire PACs: Buying Political Immunity

American democracy is increasingly a playground for the ultra-wealthy. While ordinary citizens struggle to make their voices heard, a small cabal of billionaires has seized the levers of political power, leveraging vast fortunes to shape policy, rewrite laws, and secure immunity from accountability. In the 2024 election cycle, 150 billionaire families spent a record $1.9 billion to influence federal elections, targeting tax policy, deregulation, and labor laws that directly affect their bottom lines (Americans for Tax Fairness, 2024)[xxv][xxvii]. This article explores the mechanics, consequences, and implications of billionaire PACs, focusing on the unprecedented influence of figures like Elon Musk and the staggering returns on their political investments.

1. The $1.9 Billion Election Takeover

The Scale of Billionaire Influence

The 2024 election marked a watershed moment for billionaire political spending. With a week to go before Election Day, just 150 billionaire families had already shattered previous records by contributing $1.9 billion to federal campaigns—nearly 60% more than the $1.2 billion spent by over 600 individual billionaires in 2020 (Americans for Tax Fairness, 2024). This tidal wave of cash was directed overwhelmingly toward super PACs, which, thanks to the Supreme Court's Citizens United decision, can accept unlimited contributions from individuals and corporations (Campaign Legal Center, 2025)[xxviii].

Targeting Policy: Taxes, Deregulation, and Labor

Billionaire-funded PACs do not simply back candidates; they shape the political agenda. The vast majority of this spending was aimed at advancing policies that benefit the ultra-wealthy, including tax cuts, deregulation, and weakening labor protections (Americans for Tax Fairness, 2024). In key Senate races, billionaire contributions accounted for more than half of all outside spending, tipping the balance of power in favor of candidates who promised to deliver on these priorities (Americans for Tax Fairness, 2024).

Partisan Breakdown

The spending was heavily skewed toward the Republican Party. Over two-thirds (70%) of billionaire-family contributions went to committees backing GOP candidates and conservative causes, while less than a quarter (23%) supported Democratic hopefuls (Americans for Tax Fairness, 2024). The remainder went to independent candidates and issue-based committees, such as those advocating for cryptocurrency or the state of Israel.

2. Elon Musk's Hostile Takeover

The Largest Donor in History

Elon Musk, the world's richest person, was the single largest donor in the 2024 election cycle, spending at least $277 million to back President-elect Donald Trump and other Republican candidates (CBS News, 2024)[xxix]. Musk's contributions alone represented close to 2% of all election spending by candidates, parties, and committees across all federal elections (Americans for Tax Fairness, 2024).

Infiltrating the Treasury

Musk's political investments were not limited to campaign contributions. In the wake of Trump's election, Musk and his allies sought unprecedented access to federal agencies, including the Treasury Department. Reports indicate that Musk's team lobbied for direct access to taxpayer data and financial systems, ostensibly to "streamline" government operations but raising serious concerns about privacy and abuse of power (Americans for Tax Fairness, 2024).

Lobbying Against Labor

Musk's influence extended to labor policy, where he aggressively lobbied against unionization efforts in the automotive sector. His companies, including Tesla and SpaceX, have long resisted worker organizing, and his political spending was aimed at ensuring that anti-union policies remained in place (Americans for Tax Fairness, 2024).

3. Policy ROI: $130+ in Tax Breaks for Every $1 Spent

The Lobbying Investment

The returns on billionaire political investments are staggering. Research shows that for every $1 spent on lobbying and campaign contributions, corporations and wealthy individuals can expect to receive $130 or more in tax breaks and regulatory benefits (Americans for Tax Fairness, 2024). This calculus makes political spending a no-brainer for oligarchs, who can recoup their investments many times over through favorable legislation and executive action.

The Trump-Musk Agenda

The second Trump administration, buoyed by billionaire donors like Musk, pursued an aggressive agenda of tax cuts, deregulation, and privatization. These policies were designed to deliver trillions in savings to the ultra-wealthy, effectively turning campaign contributions into a profit center (Americans for Tax Fairness, 2024).

The Human Cost

The consequences of this quid pro quo are borne by ordinary Americans. Tax cuts for the wealthy mean fewer resources for public services, infrastructure, and social safety nets. Deregulation leads to environmental degradation, unsafe workplaces, and financial instability. Weakened labor laws erode worker protections and suppress wages.

4. The Mechanics of Billionaire PACs

Super PACs and Dark Money

The vast majority of billionaire political spending flows through super PACs, which can raise and spend unlimited sums on behalf of candidates and causes (OpenSecrets, 2024)[xxx]. These groups are ostensibly independent of campaigns, but in practice, they are deeply intertwined with the candidates they support (Americans for Tax Fairness, 2024).

Dark Money Networks

In addition to super PACs, billionaires also channel funds through so-called "dark money" groups—nonprofits and shell companies that do not disclose their donors (Brennan Center, 2025)[xxxi]. These groups spent a record $1.9 billion in the 2024 cycle, further obscuring the sources of political influence (Brennan Center, 2025).

The Role of Family Offices

Billionaire families often use sophisticated "family office" structures to coordinate their political giving, allowing them to maximize their impact while minimizing scrutiny (Americans for Tax Fairness, 2024).

5. The Consequences for Democracy

Drowning Out Ordinary Voices

The flood of billionaire money into politics has a chilling effect on democracy. Ordinary citizens, who lack the resources to compete with billionaire-funded campaigns, are effectively shut out of the political process (Americans for Tax Fairness, 2024). This dynamic undermines the principle of "one person, one vote," replacing it with a system where wealth equals influence.

Policy Capture

The policy agenda is increasingly driven by the interests of the ultra-wealthy, rather than the needs of the broader public. Tax policy, labor law, environmental regulation, and financial oversight are all shaped by the preferences of a tiny elite (Americans for Tax Fairness, 2024).

Erosion of Trust

The perception that government is "for sale" to the highest bidder erodes public trust in democratic institutions. When billionaires can buy political immunity, faith in the fairness and integrity of the system collapses (Americans for Tax Fairness, 2024).

6. The Role of Citizens United

Unleashing the Floodgates

The Supreme Court's 2010 Citizens United decision is widely seen as the turning point in the rise of billionaire political power. By allowing corporations and individuals to spend unlimited sums on independent political expenditures, the decision opened the floodgates to a new era of oligarchic influence (Campaign Legal Center, 2025).

The Explosion of Spending

Since Citizens United, billionaire political spending has increased 160-fold, from just $16 million in 2008 to over $2.6 billion in 2024 (Americans for Tax Fairness, 2024). This explosion of cash has transformed American politics, making it increasingly difficult for candidates without billionaire backing to compete.

7. The Human Face of Oligarchy

Case Studies in Influence

Elon Musk is not alone in his quest for political power. Other billionaires, such as Linda McMahon and Howard Lutnick, have used their fortunes to secure high-level government positions and shape policy in their favor (Americans for Tax Fairness, 2024). McMahon, for example, was appointed Secretary of Education after donating $25 million to GOP candidates, while Lutnick became Commerce Secretary after contributing $21 million (Americans for Tax Fairness, 2024).

The Price of Access

The revolving door between billionaire donors and government is a hallmark of modern American politics. Those who write the biggest checks are rewarded with access, influence, and, in some cases, direct control over policy (Americans for Tax Fairness, 2024).

8. The Fight for Reform

Public Financing Solutions

Some states, such as New York, have experimented with public financing programs that allow candidates to raise competitive amounts from small donors, rather than relying on billionaire megadonors (Brennan Center, 2025)[xxxii]. These programs aim to level the playing field and reduce the influence of the ultra-wealthy.

Legislative Proposals

Advocates for reform have called for a range of measures, including stricter limits on campaign contributions, greater transparency for dark money groups, and stronger enforcement of existing laws (Brennan Center, 2025). These reforms are essential to restoring the integrity of American democracy.

The Challenge Ahead

Despite growing public awareness of the problem, the power of billionaire PACs continues to grow. Until meaningful reforms are enacted, the voices of ordinary Americans will remain drowned out by the cacophony of oligarchic influence.

The rise of billionaire PACs represents a fundamental threat to American democracy. By flooding campaigns with cash, the ultra-wealthy have bought themselves political immunity, shaping policy to serve their interests at the expense of the broader public. The returns on their investments are staggering—every dollar spent on lobbying and campaign contributions yields $130 or more in tax breaks and regulatory benefits (Americans for Tax Fairness, 2024). The consequences for democracy, trust, and equality are profound.

Globalization Grift: Exploitation Without Borders

The promise of globalization was once heralded as a tide that would lift all boats, spreading prosperity and opportunity across the world. In reality, the global economy has become a rigged game, with multinational corporations and billionaire elites extracting wealth from nations and workers alike, while evading taxes, exploiting labor, and redefining "development" as a process of extraction rather than empowerment. This article examines the mechanics and consequences of this global grift, focusing on how Apple and Nike shelter $245 billion in profits offshore, how Walmart and Tesla exploit vulnerable workers in the Global South, and how the myth of wealth creation obscures a reality of overexploitation.

1. Offshore Tax Havens: Starving Public Coffers

The Scale of the Problem

Apple and Nike are among the world's most admired brands, but their financial practices tell a different story. Leaked documents from the Paradise Papers reveal that Apple alone has parked over $252 billion in

51

profits offshore, while Nike has sheltered billions more in tax havens like the Netherlands and Bermuda[xxxiii][xxxiv][xxxv]. Combined, these companies have shielded roughly $245 billion in profits from taxation, depriving governments of vital revenue for public services and infrastructure[xxxvi].

How the Scheme Works

Apple's strategy is emblematic of the global tax avoidance playbook. After facing scrutiny for its use of Irish subsidiaries to minimize its tax bill, Apple's advisers sought out new havens, ultimately settling on Jersey, a tiny island in the English Channel that charges no tax on corporate profits for most companies. There, Apple established new corporate structures that allowed it to continue paying ultra-low tax rates on the majority of its global profits[xxxvii].

Nike, meanwhile, shifted its valuable trademarks to Dutch subsidiaries, enabling it to channel royalty payments through the Netherlands, where it pays little or no tax on these earnings[xxxviii]. The Paradise Papers show that both companies relied on top law firms and offshore service providers to set up and administer these complex structures.

The Consequences

The impact of these schemes is profound. By shifting profits to tax havens, Apple and Nike have avoided paying billions in taxes to the United States and other countries where they operate[xxxix]. This deprives governments of revenue needed for education, healthcare, and social services, effectively forcing ordinary citizens to shoulder a greater tax burden.

2. Sweatshop Economics: Exploiting the Global South

Walmart and Child Labor in Bangladesh

Walmart, the world's largest retailer, has long been criticized for its reliance on sweatshop labor in countries like Bangladesh. Investigations have revealed that children as young as 10 work in factories supplying Walmart, often for less than $2 a day and under dangerous conditions[xl]. These workers produce cheap goods for Western consumers, while Walmart reaps massive profits and resists efforts to improve labor standards.

Tesla and Cobalt Mining in the Congo

Tesla, the electric vehicle pioneer, is equally implicated in the exploitation of the Global South. The company's supply chain depends on cobalt, a key component of lithium-ion batteries. Most of the world's cobalt is mined in the Democratic Republic of Congo, where child labor, unsafe working conditions, and environmental degradation are rampant. Despite promises to address these issues, Tesla and other tech giants continue to source cobalt from mines where workers—many of them children—toil for pennies a day.

The Human Cost

The human cost of these practices is staggering. Workers in Bangladesh and the Congo face injury, illness, and even death, all while earning poverty wages. The profits generated by their labor flow to shareholders and executives in the Global North, while local communities are left with little to show for their sacrifices.

3. "Development" as Extraction: The Myth of Wealth Creation

Michael Parenti's Lens

Political economist Michael Parenti[xli] argues that the global economy is structured not to create wealth, but to extract it from the Global South and concentrate it in the hands of a small elite in the Global North. According to Parenti, multinational corporations and billionaire investors do not "create" wealth so much as they overexploit labor and resources, siphoning off value from the communities and countries where they operate.

The Reality of "Investment"

Foreign direct investment is often touted as a driver of development, but in practice, it frequently results in the extraction of resources and profits, with little lasting benefit for local populations. Multinational corporations set up factories and mines, pay low wages, and repatriate profits to their home countries, leaving behind environmental degradation, social dislocation, and economic dependency.

The Role of Global Institutions

International financial institutions like the World Bank and the International Monetary Fund (IMF) have facilitated this process by pressuring developing countries to adopt policies that favor foreign investors and multinational corporations. These policies often include tax breaks, deregulation, and the suppression of labor rights, further entrenching patterns of exploitation and inequality.

4. The Legal and Regulatory Landscape

The Failure of Reform

Despite repeated scandals and public outcry, efforts to curb tax avoidance and labor exploitation have been largely ineffective. The Paradise Papers and other leaks have exposed the extent of the problem, but governments have been slow to act. In some cases, new laws and regulations have been undermined by corporate lobbying and the complexity of global financial structures[xlii].

The Role of Law Firms and Consultants

Top law firms and financial consultants play a key role in facilitating tax avoidance and labor exploitation. These professionals design complex corporate structures, negotiate sweetheart deals with governments, and help multinational corporations navigate—and often circumvent—regulatory frameworks.

5. The Impact on Inequality

Widening the Gap

Globalization grift has exacerbated inequality both within and between countries. While multinational corporations and billionaire investors amass unprecedented wealth, workers in the Global South are trapped in poverty, and public services in the Global North are starved of revenue. The result is a world where the rich get richer, and the poor get poorer.

The Erosion of Democracy

The concentration of wealth and power in the hands of a global elite also undermines democracy. Multinational corporations and billionaire donors wield outsized influence over governments and policymakers, shaping laws and regulations to serve their interests. This dynamic erodes public trust in institutions and weakens the ability of citizens to hold power to account.

6. Resistance and Reform

Grassroots Movements

Despite the odds, workers and activists around the world are fighting back. Labor unions, human rights organizations, and grassroots movements are demanding better wages, safer working conditions, and an end to tax avoidance. These efforts have led to some victories, but the scale of the challenge remains immense.

Policy Solutions

Meaningful reform will require bold action at the national and international levels. Governments must close tax loopholes, strengthen labor protections, and hold multinational corporations accountable for abuses in their supply chains[xliii]. International cooperation is essential to prevent companies from simply shifting their operations to countries with weaker regulations.

7. The Myth of Corporate Social Responsibility

Greenwashing and Reputation Management

Many multinational corporations have adopted the language of corporate social responsibility (CSR), touting their commitment to sustainability, fair labor practices, and ethical sourcing. In practice, however, these initiatives are often little more than public relations exercises, designed to deflect criticism and maintain access to markets and resources.

The Need for Accountability

Real change will require more than voluntary codes of conduct and glossy CSR reports. Governments, consumers, and investors must demand transparency, accountability, and enforceable standards for corporate behavior.

8. The Future of Globalization

A Fork in the Road

The global economy stands at a crossroads. One path leads to continued exploitation, inequality, and environmental degradation. The other offers the possibility of a more just and sustainable world, where wealth is shared, workers are respected, and public services are adequately funded.

The Role of Citizens

Ultimately, the future of globalization will be shaped by the actions of citizens, workers, and policymakers. By demanding accountability, supporting ethical businesses, and advocating for reform, we can begin to dismantle the structures of exploitation and build a more equitable global economy.

The globalization grift is not an accident or a side effect of economic progress—it is the result of deliberate choices by multinational corporations, billionaire investors, and the policymakers who enable them. Apple and Nike's offshore tax avoidance, Walmart and Tesla's exploitation of vulnerable workers, and the myth of wealth creation all serve to enrich a tiny elite at the expense of the many.

The Meritocracy Myth: Luck, Privilege, and The Birth Lottery

The myth of meritocracy—the idea that success is solely the result of hard work and talent—has long been central to the American narrative. Yet, for the ultra-wealthy, this myth often obscures a far simpler truth: wealth begets wealth, and privilege is often inherited, not earned. This article dismantles the "self-made" legend by examining the data behind wealth accumulation, contrasting sanitized origin stories of billionaires like Steve Jobs and Elon Musk, and exposing the staggering arithmetic of inequality.

1. Bootstraps or Silver Spoons? The Data

The Forbes 400: A Birthright Club

A landmark 2020 study found that 70% of individuals on the Forbes 400 list inherited substantial wealth or grew up in affluent households (Forbes, 2020[xliv]). Only 21% came from middle-class backgrounds, and a mere 9% from working-class or impoverished families. This data underscores a systemic reality: the wealthiest Americans are overwhelmingly beneficiaries of preexisting advantages, not rags-to-riches strivers.

The Three Tiers of Wealth

1. Dynastic Wealth (30%): Inherited fortunes from family empires (e.g., the Waltons, Kochs).
2. Affluent Upbringing (40%): Born into upper-middle-class or wealthy families with access to elite education, networks, and seed capital.
3. True Self-Made (9%): Rose from poverty or lower-middle-class origins.

This hierarchy reveals that meritocracy is the exception, not the rule, among the economic elite.

2. The "Self-Made" Lie: Case Studies in Privilege

Steve Jobs: The Myth of the Garage Startup

Steve Jobs is frequently mythologized as a self-made genius who built Apple in his parents' garage. The reality is more nuanced:
- Adoptive Father: Paul Jobs, a machinist and Coast Guard veteran, provided a stable middle-class upbringing in Silicon Valley.
- Early Access: Jobs attended Homestead High School, a well-funded public school in Cupertino, and befriended Steve Wozniak,

whose engineering skills were critical to Apple's founding.

- Privilege of Timing: Apple's rise coincided with the 1970s tech boom, fueled by government-funded research and venture capital networks inaccessible to most Americans.

While Jobs demonstrated vision and drive, his story is one of leveraged opportunities, not solitary genius.

Elon Musk: The Emerald Mine Heir

Elon Musk's origin story is often scrubbed of its most critical detail: his family's apartheid-era wealth. Key facts:

- Father's Wealth: Errol Musk owned shares in an emerald mine in Zambia during the 1980s, generating millions in untaxed income (Business Insider, 2024[xlv]).

- Early Capital: Musk used $28,000 from his father (equivalent to $75,000 today) to co-found Zip2, his first company (CNBC, 2024[xlvi]).

- Government Subsidies: Tesla and SpaceX received over $38 billion in public funding, tax credits, and contracts (Good Jobs First, 2025[xlvii]).

Musk's narrative of "self-made" success ignores the intergenerational wealth and state support that enabled his rise.

The Narrative Sanitization Playbook

Media and corporate PR teams routinely:
- Erase Family Wealth: Framing trust-fund babies as "entrepreneurs."
- Overemphasize Struggle: Highlighting minor hardships (e.g., Musk's "sleeping in the office" anecdotes) while omitting financial safety nets.
- Celebrate "Grit": Attributing success to personal traits rather than systemic advantages.

3. The Math of Inequality: A $15/hr Worker vs. Musk's Daily Wealth

The Numbers

- Elon Musk's Daily Wealth Growth: Approximately $2 billion (Forbes, 2024).
- $15/hr Worker's Daily Earnings: $120 (before taxes, working 8 hours).

The Calculation

To earn Musk's daily wealth increase, a $15/hr worker would need:
$$\frac{2,000,000,000}{120} = 16,666,666.67 \text{ days} \approx 45,662 \text{ years}$$

$$

This figure—45,662 years—exceeds recorded human history. Even if rounded conservatively to 4,000 years (as cited in public discourse), the disparity remains incomprehensible.

Systemic Implications

- Wealth Concentration: The top 1% holds 38% of U.S. wealth, while the bottom 50% holds 2% (Federal Reserve, 2023).
- Tax Code Bias: Billionaires pay an effective tax rate of 1–3%, compared to 13–14% for median workers (ProPublica, 2021[xlviii]).

4. The Birth Lottery: How Privilege Compounds

The Inheritance Advantage

- Trust Funds: The average inheritance for the top 1% is $719,000, vs. $9,700 for the bottom 50% (Federal Reserve, 2023[xlix]).
- Education: Children of the wealthy are 8x more likely to attend Ivy League schools (Opportunity Insights, 2023).
- Networks: Affluent families provide access to internships, venture capitalists, and political influence.

The Stepped-Up Basis Loophole

When assets are inherited, their cost basis is "stepped up" to market value, erasing capital gains taxes on decades of appreciation. This loophole saves billionaire heirs $40 billion annually (Congressional Joint Committee on Taxation, 2024[1]).

5. Reclaiming the Narrative

Policy Solutions

1. Tax Unrealized Gains: Implement a billionaire tax on wealth growth, not just income.
2. Close the Stepped-Up Basis Loophole: Ensure inherited wealth is taxed fairly.
3. Invest in Public Goods: Universal childcare, education, and healthcare to level the playing field.

Cultural Shifts

- Media Accountability: Reject "self-made" myths and investigate wealth origins.
- Worker Power: Strengthen unions and wage laws to reduce inequality.

The meritocracy myth is a seductive lie that justifies inequality and absolves the power of accountability. By confronting the data—the 70% inheritance rate among billionaires, the sanitized origin stories, and the arithmetic of exploitation—we can dismantle the narratives that sustain systemic privilege. True equity requires not celebrating "self-made" billionaires but challenging the structures that allow wealth to concentrate in the hands of a birthright few.

Racialized Exploitation: Billionaires Built on Backs of Black and Brown Labor

The fortunes of America's wealthiest individuals—Jeff Bezos, Elon Musk, and the Walton family—are often celebrated as triumphs of innovation and entrepreneurship. Yet these narratives obscure a darker truth: their empires are built on systemic racialized exploitation. From Amazon's injury-plagued warehouses in Black neighborhoods to telecom giants' reliance on prison labor and Walmart's underpaid women-dominated workforce, billionaires have perfected a model of extraction that disproportionately burdens Black, Brown, and female workers. This article exposes how racial, and gender hierarchies are engineered to maximize corporate profits while trapping marginalized communities into cycles of poverty and risk.

1. Amazon's Injury Epidemic: Race, Quotas, and Bodily Sacrifice

Warehouses in Black Neighborhoods, 50% Higher Injury Rates

Amazon's logistics empire thrives on speed, surveillance, and racialized labor practices. In New York State, Amazon's self-reported data reveals a 64% surge in worker injuries from 2020 to 2021, with injury rates reaching 9.0 per 100 workers—far exceeding the national warehouse average[li]. These hazards are concentrated in facilities located in predominantly Black neighborhoods. In Minnesota, Amazon's Shakopee fulfillment center—where Black workers comprise 38% of the warehouse workforce but only 8% of the broader Twin Cities population—reported the state's highest injury rate in 2020[lii].

The Algorithmic Quota System

Black and Brown workers face harsher productivity quotas, enforced by AI-powered surveillance systems that track their every move. At the Shakopee facility, Black workers earn just 63% of white workers' wages despite similar roles, a disparity tied to discriminatory promotion practices and the relegation of workers of color to the most dangerous tasks. Nationally, Amazon's lowest-paid hourly jobs are staffed by over 60% Black and Hispanic workers, while corporate and tech roles remain 82% white or Asian[liii].

Corporate Gaslighting

Amazon dismisses these disparities as artifacts of federal reporting guidelines, claiming its warehouses offer "opportunities" for advancement [2]. Yet internal documents reveal a deliberate strategy: target communities of color for warehouse construction, exploit systemic inequities to suppress wages, and discard injured workers through triple-digit turnover rates.

2. Prison Labor Pipelines: Modern-Day Convict Leasing

AT&T's $0.20/Hour Tech Support

Telecom giants like AT&T subcontract prison labor to cut costs and undermine unions. In Colorado, Oregon, and five other states, incarcerated workers—disproportionately Black and Latino—are paid $2 per day to pose as AT&T representatives, cold-calling businesses to sell services[liv]. This system mirrors 19th-century convict leasing, where Southern states profited by renting out Black prisoners to private companies after Reconstruction.

Kickbacks and Captive Markets

Prison telecom firms like Unibase, backed by private equity, charge incarcerated people up to $2.36 per song on state-issued devices while funneling kickbacks to corrections departments[lv]. Despite Minnesota's 2023 reforms making prison calls free, the state still collected $3 million in 2024 from commissions on money transfers and entertainment services controlled by telecom monopolies.

The Thirteenth Amendment's Legacy

The 13th Amendment's exclusion of incarcerated people from slavery protections enables this exploitation. As prison populations ballooned under racist drug laws, corporations seized a captive workforce: today, 76% of prison laborers are people of color, paid pennies for jobs that once provided union wages[lvi].

3. Gender Pay Gaps: Underpaid Women Fuel Retail Profits

Walmart's 70% Women Workforce, Poverty Wages

Women comprise 54% of Walmart's U.S. workforce but face systemic underpayment and stalled mobility. In 2021, women made up just 49.8% of new hires amid a 1% decline in female employment—a disparity exacerbated by pandemic caregiving burdens[lvii]. While Walmart touts a $15 average wage, full-time female employees earn $1,200 less annually than male counterparts, with Black and Latina women at the bottom.

Amazon's Invisible Women

At Amazon, women dominate low-wage logistics roles but hold only 34% of corporate officer positions. During the pandemic, as Bezos' wealth grew by $86 billion, workers like Jennifer Bates—a Black mother and Bessemer warehouse organizer—testified to Congress about rationing insulin and living paycheck-to-paycheck.

The SEC vs. Amazon's Pay Secrecy

In 2024, the Securities and Exchange Commission (SEC) rebuked Amazon for refusing to disclose gender pay gaps, calling equity a "significant social policy issue"[lviii]. Internal documents reveal executives feared transparency would worsen Amazon's "reputational issues" tied to union-busting and warehouse conditions.

4. Historical Continuums: From Plantations to Warehouses

Convict Leasing 2.0

The racialized exploitation of prison labor today is a direct descendant of post-Civil War convict leasing, where Black men were arrested in masse and "leased" to railroads, mines, and plantations. As scholar Matthew J. Mancini notes, this system's brutality stemmed from its profit motive: "The lessee had no investment in the convict's life, only their labor". Modern telecom giants replicate this model, treating incarcerated workers as disposable.

The Plantation-to-Warehouse Pipeline

Amazon's warehouse locations map onto historic Black agricultural communities in the South and Midwest. By targeting these areas for fulfillment centers, Amazon leverages systemic disinvestment to suppress wages and weaken labor resistance—a 21st-century iteration of sharecropping economics.

5. Corporate PR vs. Reality

"Racial Equity" as Branding

Amazon and Walmart tout diversity initiatives, such as doubling Black executives (from 39 to 98 in 2020). Yet these gains mask the exploitation of frontline workers: while Bezos funds STEM scholarships, his company's injury rates in Black communities soar.

Union-Busting as Racial Violence

The crushing of the Bessemer union drive—where 80% of workers were Black—exposed how anti-union tactics disproportionately harm communities of color. Captive-audience meetings and retaliatory firings echo Jim Crow-era voter suppression.

6. Toward Liberation: Abolitionist Economics

Decarcerating Supply Chains

Reforms like Minnesota's free prison calls show progress, but ending corporate profiteering requires abolishing prison labor exemptions in the 13th Amendment and banning subcontracting to incarcerated workers.

Worker Ownership and Reparations

Movements demand billionaires cede power: from Amazon workers advocating for board seats to reparations campaigns targeting Walmart's Walton family, whose $250 billion fortune originated in rural Black communities.

Racialized exploitation is not a bug in capitalism—it is its core feature. From Amazon's warehouses to AT&T's prison call centers, billionaires weaponize race and gender to extract wealth from those least able to resist. Dismantling these systems requires more than pay equity reports; it demands a reckoning with the convict leasing past and a future where labor justice is inseparable from racial justice.

The Philanthropy Ruse: Charity as Reputation Laundering

Philanthropy is often heralded as the ultimate act of public good—a noble redistribution of wealth from the ultra-rich to those in need. Yet, beneath the surface of charitable giving lies a more complicated reality, one in which philanthropy serves as a tool for reputation management, economic influence, and even the consolidation of power. This article examines three emblematic cases: Jeff Bezos's $100 million donation to Dolly Parton, Mark Zuckerberg's $100 million education reform initiative in Newark, and the Rockefeller Foundation's century-long legacy of philanthropy. In each case, the line between altruism and self-interest is blurred, revealing philanthropy as a means of reputation laundering and political influence.

Tax-Deductible "Generosity": Bezos' $100M "Charity" to Dolly Parton

In November 2022, Jeff Bezos awarded Dolly Parton $100 million as part of his Courage and Civility Award, ostensibly to direct to charities of her choosing (Reddit, 2022[lix]). The move was widely praised, with many lauding Parton's track record as a philanthropist and

Bezos's willingness to entrust her with such a large sum. However, a closer examination reveals a more cynical calculus at play.

Bezos's donation is structured as a tax-deductible gift, allowing him to reduce his taxable income by up to $37 million, depending on his tax bracket and the specifics of the donation (Counterpunch, 2021). This means that, far from a pure act of generosity, the donation is partially subsidized by the American taxpayer. Meanwhile, Amazon—the source of Bezos's fortune—is embroiled in a $2 billion dispute with the IRS over unpaid taxes. The parallel is striking while Bezos's personal philanthropy garners positive headlines, his company resists contributing its fair share to the public coffers.

The optics are further complicated by the fact that Amazon employees and customers—whose labor and purchases generate Bezos's wealth—are rarely acknowledged in the press releases surrounding his charitable giving (Counterpunch, 2021[lx]). This omission underscores the extent to which philanthropy is used to launder reputations, deflecting attention from corporate practices that may be less than savory.

Zuckerberg's "Education Reform": Donating to Charter Schools While Facebook Algorithms Gut Local News

Mark Zuckerberg's $100 million donation to Newark's public schools in 2010 was billed as a bold attempt to reform urban education. The initiative, led by then-Mayor Cory Booker, aimed to make Newark a model for the nation by expanding charter schools, weakening teacher tenure protections, and introducing new accountability measures (Vox, 2019[lxi]; EdWeek, 2015[lxii]).

The results, however, were mixed at best. While some schools saw improvements, the reforms also led to the closure of traditional public schools, the replacement of principals, and a shift toward privatization. Critics argue that the initiative prioritized market-based solutions over the needs of the community, ultimately undermining the public education system it purported to help (Vox, 2019).

Meanwhile, Facebook—Zuckerberg's primary source of wealth—has been accused of gutting local news through its algorithm-driven platforms. By prioritizing viral content and deprioritizing local journalism, Facebook has contributed to the decline of local newspapers, leaving many communities without reliable sources of information (US News Deserts, n.d.[lxiii]). The irony is stark: while Zuckerberg donates to education reform, his company's practices erode the civic infrastructure that underpins informed citizenship.

The Rockefeller Playbook: Philanthropy as a Justification for Monopoly Power

The Rockefeller Foundation, established in 1913, is often cited as a paragon of philanthropic virtue. Its mission is to "promote the wellbeing of humanity throughout the world," and it has disbursed over $17 billion in grants to date (Centre for Public Impact, 2025[lxiv]). Yet, the foundation's origins are inseparable from the monopoly power of Standard Oil, which was broken up by the Supreme Court in 1911 for anti-competitive practices (Centre for Public Impact, 2025).

John D. Rockefeller's philanthropy was, in part, an effort to rehabilitate his public image after years of criticism for his business practices. By founding the Rockefeller Foundation, he sought to demonstrate that his wealth could be used for the public good—even as his company's dominance stifled competition and concentrated economic power (Philanthropy Roundtable, 2023[lxv]).

The Rockefeller Foundation's focus on health, education, and social welfare was genuine in its intent, but it also served to justify the existence of vast fortunes and to forestall calls for greater regulation and redistribution. In this way, philanthropy became a tool for maintaining the status quo, allowing the ultra-wealthy to shape public policy while avoiding more radical reforms.

Philanthropy as Reputation Laundering: A Historical Perspective

The use of philanthropy to launder reputations is not a new phenomenon. From the robber barons of the Gilded Age to today's tech titans, the ultra-wealthy have long understood the power of charitable giving to deflect criticism and secure social legitimacy. As Eric Posner and Glen Weyl argue, "The great monopolies of that period—Rockefeller's Standard Oil, the sugar trust, the financial and railroad interests—used their power to corrupt the economy and politics" (Econlib, 2018[lxvi], para. 1).

Yet, the reality is more nuanced. While philanthropy can and does fund important social programs, it also allows the wealthy to shape public discourse, influence policy, and avoid accountability. The Rockefeller Foundation's work in public health, for example, has saved countless lives—but it has also helped to legitimize the concentration of wealth and power that made such philanthropy possible in the first place (Centre for Public Impact, 2025).

The Limits of Philanthropy: Who Decides the Public Good?

One of the central criticisms of elite philanthropy is that it places the power to define and address social problems in the hands of a few individuals, rather than in the hands of the public or its elected representatives. When Jeff Bezos or Mark Zuckerberg decides where to direct their charitable dollars, they are making choices that affect millions of people—choices that are not subject to democratic oversight or accountability.

This dynamic is particularly troubling in the context of education and local news. When Zuckerberg funds charter schools, he is shaping the future of public education in ways that may not align with the priorities of local communities (Vox, 2019). When Facebook's algorithms deprioritize local news, they are undermining the civic infrastructure that makes democracy possible (US News Deserts, n.d.).

Similarly, Bezos's donations may fund worthy causes, but they do not address the systemic issues—such as corporate tax avoidance—that contribute to inequality in the first place (Counterpunch, 2021).

Philanthropy and Power

Philanthropy is not inherently bad. It has funded life-saving medical research, supported education, and provided relief in times of crisis. However, it is also a powerful tool for reputation laundering, allowing the ultra-wealthy to shape public opinion, influence policy, and avoid accountability.

The cases of Jeff Bezos, Mark Zuckerberg, and the Rockefeller Foundation illustrate the dual nature of philanthropy: it can be a force for good, but it can also serve to entrench the power of the few at the expense of the many. As long as philanthropy is used to justify monopoly power, corporate tax avoidance, and the erosion of public institutions, it will remain a ruse—a way for the wealthy to launder their reputations while avoiding the hard work of building a more just and equitable society.

Reimagining Equity: Abolish Billionaires

The United States is now home to more billionaires than any other nation—902 as of 2025—and the collective wealth of its wealthiest individuals far exceeds the GDP of most countries[lxvii][lxviii]. Yet, this unprecedented concentration of wealth has not translated into shared prosperity. Instead, it has fueled historic inequality, eroded public trust, and hollowed out the middle class[lxix][lxx][lxxi]. This article argues that to reimagine equity, we must abolish the billionaire class by closing tax loopholes, mandating worker ownership, and redirecting public subsidies to community-controlled assets. Only by dismantling the structures that enable extreme wealth accumulation can we build a fairer, more democratic society.

The Billionaire Paradox: Wealth Without Limit

The Scale of American Oligarchy

The U.S. leads the world with 902 billionaires, who collectively control over $6 trillion in wealth. The top 12 American billionaires alone are worth more than $2 trillion—a sum that has nearly tripled since

2020[lxxii]. This wealth is concentrated in the hands of a tiny elite, while 36 million Americans live in poverty and millions more struggle to afford basic necessities. The result is a society where the richest can buy political influence, shape policy, and insulate themselves from the consequences of their actions.

The Myth of Meritocracy

Despite popular narratives of self-made success, the vast majority of billionaires inherited wealth or grew up in affluent households. Their fortunes are often built on government subsidies, tax breaks, and the exploitation of workers—not just individual genius or hard work. The rise of the billionaire class is a symptom of a broken system, not a sign of its health.

Close the Loopholes: Tax Unrealized Gains, End Stepped-Up Basis, and Fund IRS Audits

The Tax Avoidance Playbook

Billionaires exploit legal loopholes to avoid paying their fair share. By holding onto assets and borrowing against their value, they defer or entirely avoid capital gains taxes. When they die, their heirs inherit these assets at their current market value—a process known as the "stepped-up basis" loophole—which erases billions in potential tax liability[lxxiii].

Taxing Unrealized Gains

To close these loopholes, we must tax unrealized capital gains. This would require billionaires to pay taxes on the annual increase in the value of their assets, not just when they sell them. Such a policy would capture wealth as it accrues, preventing the ultra-rich from deferring taxes indefinitely.

Ending the Stepped-Up Basis Loophole

Eliminating the stepped-up basis would ensure that inherited wealth is taxed fairly. Currently, heirs pay no capital gains tax on the appreciation of inherited assets, allowing dynastic wealth to grow unchecked. Closing this loophole would generate billions in revenue for public services and reduce intergenerational inequality.

Funding the IRS

The IRS has been systematically defunded, making it easier for the wealthy to evade taxes. Increasing funding for IRS enforcement would allow the agency to audit high-income individuals and corporations, recover lost revenue, and restore fairness to the tax system.

Worker Ownership: Mandate Profit-Sharing and Union Board Seats

The Power of Profit-Sharing

Worker ownership is a proven model for reducing inequality and increasing productivity. Requiring companies to share 40% of profits with employees would ensure that workers benefit directly from the wealth they create. This policy would raise wages, reduce turnover, and foster a sense of shared purpose.

Union Representation on Boards

Mandating union representation on corporate boards would give workers a voice in company decisions. In countries like Germany, where worker representatives hold up to half of board seats, companies are more stable, productive, and responsive to employee needs. Bringing this model to the U.S. would shift power from shareholders to workers and help prevent the kind of reckless decision-making that led to the 2008 financial crisis.

The Case for Co-Determination

Co-determination—the practice of giving workers and unions equal say in corporate governance—has been shown to reduce layoffs, improve wages, and increase innovation. By institutionalizing worker power, we can rebalance the economy and ensure that prosperity is shared.

Public Wealth Funds: Redirect Subsidies to Community-Owned Assets

The Subsidy Scandal

Every year, the U.S. government hands out billions in subsidies to corporations and billionaires—$38 billion to Elon Musk's companies alone. These public funds are often used to enrich shareholders rather than benefit the broader community.

Community-Owned Renewables

Redirecting subsidies to community-owned renewable energy projects would democratize access to clean power and create local jobs. Publicly owned wind and solar farms could generate revenue for municipalities, reduce energy costs, and accelerate the transition to a sustainable economy.

Affordable Housing and Healthcare

Subsidies should also be used to fund affordable housing and healthcare. Public wealth funds could finance the construction of social housing, support community health clinics, and provide universal access to essential services. These investments would reduce inequality, improve quality of life, and strengthen social cohesion.

The Alaska Model

Alaska's Permanent Fund, which distributes oil revenues to all residents, is a model for how public wealth can be shared equitably. Expanding this approach to other sectors—such as energy, housing, and healthcare—would ensure that everyone benefits from the nation's wealth, not just a privileged few.

The Global Context: Learning from Abroad

International Examples

Countries like Norway and Singapore have successfully used public wealth funds to invest in infrastructure, education, and social services. Norway's sovereign wealth fund, built on oil revenues, is now the largest in the world and provides a financial cushion for future generations. These models show that public ownership and shared prosperity are not only possible but effective.

The Limits of Philanthropy

Billionaire philanthropy is often touted as a solution to inequality, but it is no substitute for systemic reform. Private foundations are undemocratic, unaccountable, and often serve the interests of their donors rather than the public. True equity requires collective action and public control over resources.

The Political Challenge: Overcoming Oligarchic Power

The Influence of Wealth

Billionaires use their fortunes to shape policy[lxxiv], fund political campaigns, and lobby for favorable laws. This outsized influence distorts democracy and makes it harder to enact reforms that benefit the majority.

Building a Movement for Equity

To overcome this power, we need a broad-based movement for economic justice. This movement must include workers, unions, community organizations, and progressive politicians. By uniting around a shared vision of equity, we can challenge the billionaire class and demand a fairer distribution of wealth and power.

The Economic Benefits of Abolishing Billionaires

Reducing Inequality

Abolishing the billionaire class would dramatically reduce wealth inequality, which is now higher in the U.S. than in any other major developed nation. By taxing extreme wealth, sharing profits with workers, and investing in public goods, we can create a more balanced and inclusive economy.

Strengthening Democracy

Extreme wealth concentration undermines democracy by giving a tiny elite disproportionate influence over politics and policy. By redistributing power and resources, we can restore faith in democratic institutions and ensure that the government serves the many, not the few.

Promoting Stability

Worker ownership and public wealth funds create more resilient economies. When workers have a stake in their companies and communities have control over essential services, societies are better equipped to weather economic shocks and adapt to change.

The Moral Imperative

Justice and Fairness

Abolishing billionaires is not just an economic or political issue—it is a moral imperative. No individual needs or deserves a personal fortune that rivals the GDP of small nations, especially when millions struggle to meet basic needs. True justice requires that we share the fruits of our collective labor and ensure that everyone has the opportunity to thrive.

Intergenerational Equity

Extreme wealth accumulation also threatens intergenerational equity. By closing tax loopholes and redirecting subsidies to public goods, we can ensure that future generations inherit a fairer, more sustainable world.

A Future Without Billionaires

The abolition of the billionaire class is not a radical idea—it is a necessary step toward a more just and equitable society. By closing tax loopholes, mandating worker ownership, and redirecting public subsidies to community-controlled assets, we can dismantle the structures that enable extreme wealth accumulation and build a future where prosperity is shared by all.

The United States is the wealthiest nation in history,

but its riches are concentrated in the hands of a tiny elite. It is time to reimagine equity, reclaim our democracy, and abolish billionaires for good.

The Author

Juan Ramon Rodulfo Moya, **Defined by Nature**: Inhabitant of Planet Earth, Human, Son of Eladio Rodulfo and Briceida Moya, Brother of Gabriela, Gustavo and Katiuska, Father of Gabriel and Sofia; **Defined by society**: Venezuelan Citizen (Limited Human Rights by default), Friend of many, enemy of few, Neighbor, Student/Teacher/Student, Worker/Supervisor/Manager/Leader/Worker, Husband of K/Ex-Husband of K/Husband of Y; **Defined by the U.S. Immigration Office**: Legal Alien; **Classroom studies**: Master's Degree in Human Resource Management, English, Mandarin Chinese; **Real-World Studies**: Human Behavior; **Home Studios**: SEO Webmaster, Graphic Design, Application and Website Development, Internet and Social Media Marketing, Video Production, YouTube Branding, Part 107 Commercial Drone Pilot, Import-Export, Affiliate Marketing, Cooking, Laundry, Home Cleaning; **Work experience**: Public-Private-Entrepreneurial Sectors; **Other definitions:** Bitcoin Evangelist, Human Rights, Peace and Love Advocate.

Publications:

Books:

Why Maslow? How to use his theory to stay in Power Forever (2018)
¿Por qué Maslow? Cómo usar su teoría para permanecer en el Poder por siempre (2018)
Asylum Seekers (2018)
En busca de Asilo (2018)
Manual for Gorillas: 9 Rules to be the "FER-PECT" dictator (2019)
Manual para Gorilas: 9 Reglas para ser el dictador "FER-PECTO" (2019)
Why you must Play the Lottery (2019)
Por qué debes jugar la Lotería (2021)
Para Español Oprima #2: Speaking Spanish in Times of Xenophobia (2019)
Cause of Death: IGNORANCE, Human Behavior in Times of PANIC (2019)
Politics explained for Millennials, GENs XYZ and future generations (2022)
Política explicada para Millennials, GENs xyz y futuras generaciones (2022)
Las cenizas del Ejército Libertador (2023)
Remain Silent: The only right we have. The legal Aliens (2023)
Fortune Cookie Coaching 88 Motivational Tips Made of Fortune Cookies, Vol I (2024)
Vicky Erotic Tales, Vol I (2024)
TikTok Heroes in my Algorithm (2025)

AI at Home, transforming your child's Learning Experience (2025)
IA en Casa, Reinventando el aprendizaje de l@s niñ@s (2025)
Self-made billionaire in the US, Girl, hold my beer (2025)

Blogs:

Noticias de Nueva Esparta, Ubuntu Café, Coffee Secrets, Rodulfox, Red Wasp Drone, Barista Pro, Gorila Travel, Fortune Cookie Coach, All Books, Vicky Toys.

Audiovisual Productions:

Podcasts:

Ubuntu Cafe | Vicky Erotic Tales | Fortune Cookie Coach | All Books, available at: juanrodulfo.com/podcasts

Music:

Albums: Margarita | Race to Extinction | Relaxed Panda | Amazonia | Cassiopeia | Caracas | Arcoiris Musical | Close Your Eyes, available at: juanrodulfo.com/music

Photography & Video:

On sale at Adobe Stock, iStock, Shutterstock, and Veectezy, available at: juanrodulfo.com/gallery

Social Media Profiles:

BlueSky / Twitter / FB / Instagram / TikTok/ VK / LinkedIn / Sina Weibo: @rodulfox

Google Author: https://g.co/kgs/grjtN5
Google Artist: https://g.co/kgs/H7Fiqg
Twitter: https://twitter.com/rodulfox
Facebook: https://facebook.com/rodulfox
LinkedIn: https://www.linkedin.com/in/rodulfox
Instagram: https://www.instagram.com/rodulfox/
VK: https://vk.com/rodulfox
TikTok: https://www.tiktok.com/@rodulfox
Trading View: https://www.tradingview.com/u/rodulfox/

Table of Contents

- Preface 7
- The Tax Code Loophole Playbook: How Billionaires Pay Less Than You 11
- 1. Wealth vs. Income: The Legal Distinction ... 11
- 2. The Buy-Borrow-Die Strategy 12
  - Buy 12
  - Borrow 12
  - Die 13
- 3. Case Studies: Elon Musk and Larry Ellison 13
  - Elon Musk 13
  - Larry Ellison 14
- 4. Other Tax Avoidance Tactics 14
  - Real Estate and Depreciation 14
  - Charitable Donations and Foundations 15
  - Business Expenses 15
- 5. Policy Failure: Decades of Tax Cuts and IRS Defunding 15
  - The Shift Toward Inequality 15
  - Defunding the IRS 16
  - The Medicare Tax Loophole 16
- 6. The Human Cost: Inequality and the Middle Class 16
  - The Growing Wealth Gap 16

The Burden on Working Americans 17

7. Reform Proposals and Political Resistance 17
   Closing the Loopholes 17
   Political Obstacles 17

8. International Comparisons......................... 18
   Lessons from Abroad 18
   The Global Race to the Bottom 18

Welfare for the Wealthy: The $38 Billion Government Handout 19

1. Subsidy Kings: Elon Musk's $38 Billion Empire... 19
   The Scale of the Handout 19
   The Breakdown........................... 20
   The Timing 21

2. The Mechanics of Corporate Welfare 21
   Grants, Tax Credits, and Contracts 21
   The Subsidy Harvesting Strategy . 22

3. Corporate Socialism: Amazon's HQ2 and State-Funded Stadiums 22
   The HQ2 Extortion Racket........... 22
   State-Funded Stadiums................ 23

4. Privatized Gains, Socialized Losses: COVID Bailouts 24
   The Great Bailout 24

5. The Consequences of Welfare for the Wealthy 25
    Erosion of Public Trust 25
    Widening Inequality 25
    Missed Opportunities 25

6. The Political Economy of Corporate Welfare 26
    The Role of Lobbying 26
    The Myth of the Free Market 26

7. Case Studies: Musk vs. Bezos 27
    Musk's Subsidy Harvesting 27
    Bezos's Amazon Empire 27

8. The Way Forward: Reforming Corporate Welfare 27
    Transparency and Accountability 27
    Ending the Extortion Racket 28
    Prioritizing Public Goods 28

Union Busting 101: Crushing Worker Power to Maximize Profits 29

1. The Anatomy of Union Busting 29
2. Amazon's Anti-Union Toolkit 30
    Captive-Audience Meetings 30
    Retaliatory Firings and Discipline 31
    Propaganda and Division 31
    Legal and Financial Firepower 32
3. Starbucks' Union Avoidance 32

> Closing Unionized Stores 32
> Denying Benefits to Pro-Union Workers 32
> Stalling Negotiations 33

4. Walmart's Wage Suppression 33
   > Poverty Wages 33
   > Anti-Union Propaganda 34
   > High Turnover and Worker Disempowerment 34

5. The Legal Landscape 34
   > Weak Labor Laws 34
   > NLRB Challenges 35
   > Unfair Labor Practices 35

6. The Human Cost 36
   > Fear and Intimidation 36
   > Economic Insecurity 36
   > Social Division 36

7. The Broader Implications 37
   > Erosion of Worker Rights 37
   > Impact on Democracy 37
   > Global Reach 37

8. Resistance and Hope 38
   > Billionaire PACs: Buying Political Immunity 40

1. The $1.9 Billion Election Takeover 40

The Scale of Billionaire Influence 40
  Targeting Policy: Taxes, Deregulation, and Labor 41
  Partisan Breakdown 41
2. Elon Musk's Hostile Takeover 42
  The Largest Donor in History 42
  Infiltrating the Treasury............... 42
  Lobbying Against Labor 43
3. Policy ROI: $130+ in Tax Breaks for Every $1 Spent 43
  The Lobbying Investment 43
  The Trump-Musk Agenda 44
  The Human Cost........................... 44
4. The Mechanics of Billionaire PACs 45
  Super PACs and Dark Money....... 45
  Dark Money Networks 45
  The Role of Family Offices 45
5. The Consequences for Democracy.............. 46
  Drowning Out Ordinary Voices.... 46
  Policy Capture 46
  Erosion of Trust............................ 47
6. The Role of Citizens United 47
  Unleashing the Floodgates........... 47
  The Explosion of Spending 47
7. The Human Face of Oligarchy 48

  Case Studies in Influence 48
  The Price of Access 48
8. The Fight for Reform 49
  Public Financing Solutions 49
  Legislative Proposals 49
  The Challenge Ahead 49
  Globalization Grift: Exploitation Without Borders 51
1. Offshore Tax Havens: Starving Public Coffers 51
  The Scale of the Problem 51
  How the Scheme Works 52
  The Consequences 53
2. Sweatshop Economics: Exploiting the Global South 53
  Walmart and Child Labor in Bangladesh 53
  Tesla and Cobalt Mining in the Congo 54
  The Human Cost 54
3. "Development" as Extraction: The Myth of Wealth Creation 55
  Michael Parenti's Lens 55
  The Reality of "Investment" 55
  The Role of Global Institutions 56
4. The Legal and Regulatory Landscape 56

The Failure of Reform 56
The Role of Law Firms and Consultants 56
5. The Impact on Inequality 57
Widening the Gap 57
The Erosion of Democracy 57
6. Resistance and Reform 58
Grassroots Movements 58
Policy Solutions 58
7. The Myth of Corporate Social Responsibility 59
Greenwashing and Reputation Management 59
The Need for Accountability 59
8. The Future of Globalization 59
A Fork in the Road 59
The Role of Citizens 60

The Meritocracy Myth: Luck, Privilege, and The Birth Lottery 61

1. Bootstraps or Silver Spoons? The Data 61
The Forbes 400: A Birthright Club 61
The Three Tiers of Wealth 62
2. The "Self-Made" Lie: Case Studies in Privilege 62

Steve Jobs: The Myth of the Garage Startup 62
Elon Musk: The Emerald Mine Heir 63
The Narrative Sanitization Playbook 64

3. The Math of Inequality: A $15/hr Worker vs. Musk's Daily Wealth 64
The Numbers 64
The Calculation............................ 64
Systemic Implications 65

4. The Birth Lottery: How Privilege Compounds 65
The Inheritance Advantage 65
The Stepped-Up Basis Loophole .. 66

5. Reclaiming the Narrative 66
Policy Solutions 66
Cultural Shifts.............................. 66

Racialized Exploitation: Billionaires Built on Backs of Black and Brown Labor 68

1. Amazon's Injury Epidemic: Race, Quotas, and Bodily Sacrifice 69
Warehouses in Black Neighborhoods, 50% Higher Injury Rates 69
The Algorithmic Quota System 69

Corporate Gaslighting 70
2. Prison Labor Pipelines: Modern-Day Convict Leasing 70
  AT&T's $0.20/Hour Tech Support 70
    Kickbacks and Captive Markets ... 71
    The Thirteenth Amendment's Legacy 71
3. Gender Pay Gaps: Underpaid Women Fuel Retail Profits 72
    Walmart's 70% Women Workforce, Poverty Wages 72
    Amazon's Invisible Women 72
    The SEC vs. Amazon's Pay Secrecy 73
4. Historical Continuums: From Plantations to Warehouses 73
    Convict Leasing 2.0 73
    The Plantation-to-Warehouse Pipeline 74
5. Corporate PR vs. Reality 74
    "Racial Equity" as Branding 74
    Union-Busting as Racial Violence 74
6. Toward Liberation: Abolitionist Economics 75
    Decarcerating Supply Chains 75

Worker Ownership and Reparations 75

The Philanthropy Ruse: Charity as Reputation Laundering..................................... 77

Tax-Deductible "Generosity": Bezos' $100M "Charity" to Dolly Parton 77

Zuckerberg's "Education Reform": Donating to Charter Schools While Facebook Algorithms Gut Local News 79

The Rockefeller Playbook: Philanthropy as a Justification for Monopoly Power 80

Philanthropy as Reputation Laundering: A Historical Perspective 81

The Limits of Philanthropy: Who Decides the Public Good? 82

Philanthropy and Power 83

Reimagining Equity: Abolish Billionaires 84

The Billionaire Paradox: Wealth Without Limit 84

The Scale of American Oligarchy . 84

The Myth of Meritocracy 85

Close the Loopholes: Tax Unrealized Gains, End Stepped-Up Basis, and Fund IRS Audits 85

The Tax Avoidance Playbook 85

Taxing Unrealized Gains 86

Ending the Stepped-Up Basis Loophole 86

- Funding the IRS 86
- Worker Ownership: Mandate Profit-Sharing and Union Board Seats 87
  - The Power of Profit-Sharing 87
  - Union Representation on Boards. 87
  - The Case for Co-Determination .. 88
- Public Wealth Funds: Redirect Subsidies to Community-Owned Assets 88
  - The Subsidy Scandal..................... 88
  - Community-Owned Renewables. 88
  - Affordable Housing and Healthcare 89
  - The Alaska Model 89
- The Global Context: Learning from Abroad.. 90
  - International Examples............... 90
  - The Limits of Philanthropy 90
- The Political Challenge: Overcoming Oligarchic Power... 91
  - The Influence of Wealth 91
  - Building a Movement for Equity.. 91
- The Economic Benefits of Abolishing Billionaires 91
  - Reducing Inequality 91
  - Strengthening Democracy............92
  - Promoting Stability 92
- The Moral Imperative 92

- Justice and Fairness 92
- Intergenerational Equity 93
- A Future Without Billionaires 93
- The Author 96
- Publications: 97
  - Books: 97
  - Blogs: 98
- Audiovisual Productions: 98
  - Podcasts: 98
  - Music: 98
  - Photography & Video: 99
- Social Media Profiles: 99
  - Endnotes 113

Endnotes

[i] ProPublica. (2021, June 8). The Secret IRS Files: Trove of Never-Before-Seen Records Reveal How the Wealthiest Avoid Income Tax. https://www.propublica.org/article/the-secret-irs-files-trove-of-never-before-seen-records-reveal-how-the-wealthiest-avoid-income-tax

[ii] Institute on Taxation and Economic Policy (ITEP). (2023, April 15). It's Tax Day. You've Paid Your Share, but the Billionaires Haven't. https://itep.org/tax-day-billionaires-wealth-inequality-corporate-tax-avoidance/

[iii] SmartAsset. (2025, April 25). 5 Ways Billionaires Avoid Taxes: Strategies and Examples. https://smartasset.com/taxes/5-ways-billionaires-avoid-taxes-strategies-and-examples

[iv] PBS. (2025, March 12). Simple Civics | How do billionaires avoid paying taxes? https://www.pbs.org/video/how-do-billionaires-avoid-paying-taxes-5azijx/

[v] ProPublica. (2024, December 18). How Billionaires Have Sidestepped a Tax Aimed at the Rich. https://www.propublica.org/article/billionaires-net-investment-income-tax

[vi] Senator Elizabeth Warren. (2024, September 13). ICYMI: At Hearing, Warren Calls for Taxing Billionaires in 2025 to Fund Investments in High-Quality Child Care. https://www.warren.senate.gov/newsroom/press-releases/icymi-at-hearing-warren-calls-for-taxing-billionaires-in-2025-to-fund-investments-in-high-quality-child-care

[vii] CNBC. (2025, May 23). House Republican 'big beautiful' tax bill favors the rich.

https://www.cnbc.com/2025/05/23/house-republican-big-beautiful-tax-bill-favors-the-rich.html

[viii] Washington Post. (2025, February 26). Elon Musk's business empire is built on $38 billion in government contracts, loans, subsidies and tax credits. https://www.washingtonpost.com/technology/interactive/2025/elon-musk-business-government-contracts-funding/

[ix] Good Jobs First. (2025, February 28). Elon Musk's business empire is built on $38 billion in government funding. https://goodjobsfirst.org/elon-musks-business-empire-is-built-on-38-billion-in-government-funding/

[x] Fortune. (2025, March 19). The true genius of Elon Musk is his 'subsidy harvesting strategy'—Tesla, SpaceX, XAI, DOGE. https://fortune.com/2025/03/19/elon-musk-subsidy-harvesting-strategy-tesla-spacex-xai-doge/

[xi] Le Monde. (2025, February 27). Elon Musk's empire has benefited from $38 billion in contracts and government aid. https://www.lemonde.fr/en/economy/article/2025/02/27/elon-musk-s-empire-has-benefited-from-38-billion-in-contracts-and-government-aid_6738618_19.html

[xii] NPR. (2025, June 6). What the Trump-Musk breakup may mean for SpaceX and Tesla. https://www.npr.org/2025/06/06/nx-s1-5424689/elon-musk-trump-fight-subsidies-spacex-tesla

[xiii] Wired. (2025, June 6). Elon Musk's fight with Trump threatens $48 billion in federal contracts. https://www.wired.com/story/elon-musk-federal-contracts-government/

[xiv] Brookings Institution. (2019, February 14). Amazon's HQ2 is over—but the debate over incentives is not. https://www.brookings.edu/articles/amazons-hq2-is-over-but-the-debate-over-incentives-is-not/

[xv] The New York Times. (2018, November 13). How Amazon's HQ2 search became a spectacle of

corporate welfare. https://www.nytimes.com/2018/11/13/technology/amazon-hq2-subsidies.html

[xvi] Brookings Institution. (2016, September 14). Why the federal government should stop spending billions on private sports stadiums. https://www.brookings.edu/articles/why-the-federal-government-should-stop-spending-billions-on-private-sports-stadiums/

[xvii] ProPublica. (2020, July 30). Bailout Tracker: Tracking the federal government's response to the coronavirus pandemic. https://projects.propublica.org/coronavirus/bailouts/

[xviii] The Guardian. (2020, April 2). Coronavirus bailout: US firms with billions in cash got millions in small business aid. https://www.theguardian.com/world/2020/apr/02/coronavirus-bailout-us-firms-billions-cash-small-business-aid

[xix] The Atlantic. (2015, September 30). How sports stadiums became welfare for the wealthy. https://www.theatlantic.com/business/archive/2015/09/stadiums-welfare-wealthy/407830/

[xx] EPI Press. (2025, January 28). New report details how Amazon, Starbucks, and Trader Joe's have crushed worker organizing campaigns. https://www.epi.org/press/new-report-details-how-amazon-starbucks-and-trader-joes-have-crushed-worker-organizing-campaigns/

[xxi] The Nation. (2025, February 13). How Amazon is taking its union-busting to new heights. https://www.thenation.com/article/activism/amazon-union-busting-north-carolina/

[xxii] LaborLab. (2025, February 18). Amazon thrives in Trump's anti-worker America. https://laborlab.us/union-busting-without-consequences-amazon-thrives-in-trumps-anti-worker-america/

[xxiii] Economic Policy Institute (EPI). (2025, January 28). Corporate union busting in plain sight: How Amazon, Starbucks, and Trader Joe's have crushed worker organizing campaigns. https://www.epi.org/publication/corporate-union-busting/

[xxiv] Foxglove. (2025, May 9). The first British legal challenge against Amazon's union-busting. https://www.foxglove.org.uk/2025/05/09/first-british-legal-challenge-amazon-union-busting/

[xxv] UNI Global Union. (2025, Spring). Amazon Newsletter Spring 2025 – Extended Content. https://uniglobalunion.org/news/amazon-newsletter-spring-2025/

[xxvi] Americans for Tax Fairness. (2025, April 1). Billionaires buying elections: They've come to collect. https://americansfortaxfairness.org/billionaires-buying-elections-theyve-come-to-collect/

[xxvii] Americans for Tax Fairness. (2024, October 29). Billionaire clans spend nearly $2 billion on 2024 elections. https://americansfortaxfairness.org/billionaire-clans-spend-nearly-2-billion-2024-elections/

[xxviii] Campaign Legal Center. (2025, January 21). How does the Citizens United decision still affect us in 2025? https://campaignlegal.org/update/how-does-citizens-united-decision-still-affect-us-2025

[xxix] CBS News. (2024, December 6). Elon Musk spends $277 million to back Trump and Republican candidates. https://www.cbsnews.com/news/elon-musk-277-million-trump-republican-candidates-donations/

[xxx] OpenSecrets. (2024). 2024 outside spending, by super PAC. https://www.opensecrets.org/outside-spending/super_pacs

[xxxi] Brennan Center for Justice. (2025, May 7). Dark money hit a record high of $1.9 billion in 2024 federal races. https://www.brennancenter.org/our-

work/research-reports/dark-money-hit-record-high-19-billion-2024-federal-races

[xxxii] Brennan Center for Justice. (2025, February 14). New York's answer to billionaire-fueled campaigns. https://www.brennancenter.org/our-work/analysis-opinion/new-yorks-answer-billionaire-fueled-campaigns

[xxxiii] Institute on Taxation and Economic Policy (ITEP). (2017, August 2). Offshore tax avoidance. https://itep.org/tag/offshore-tax-avoidance/

[xxxiv] International Consortium of Investigative Journalists (ICIJ). (2017, November 6). Apple's secret offshore island hop revealed by Paradise Papers leak. https://www.icij.org/investigations/paradise-papers/apples-secret-offshore-island-hop-revealed-by-paradise-papers-leak-icij/

[xxxv] The Fact Coalition. (2017, November 16). Shopping for a tax haven: How Nike and Apple accelerated their tax avoidance strategies, according to Paradise Papers. https://thefactcoalition.org/shopping-tax-haven-nike-apple-accelerated-tax-avoidance-strategies-according-paradise-papers/

[xxxvi] Air Corporate. (2025, March 1). 8 juicy tax havens from around the world. https://air-corporate.com/blog/tax-havens/

[xxxvii] The New York Times. (2017, November 6). After a tax crackdown, Apple found a new shelter for its profits. https://www.nytimes.com/2017/11/06/world/apple-taxes-jersey.html

[xxxviii] International Consortium of Investigative Journalists (ICIJ). (2021, July 15). Nike fails to stop EU probe on billions in alleged tax dodging. https://www.icij.org/tags/nike/

[xxxix] Korea JoongAng Daily. (2024, September 20). Apple, McDonald's, Nike avoided taxes in 2023: NTS. https://koreajoongangdaily.joins.com/news/2024-0-20/business/finance/Foreign-corporations-avoided-Korean-taxes-in-2022-NTS/213737

[xl] Projects (Memory Entries):
- projects.tax_policy_reform (2025-06-08): Writing a book on IRS reform, focusing on tax evasion by big corporations and churches. - projects.wealth_inequality (2025-06-08): Writing a book on wealth inequality, focusing on tax policies and government subsidies for billionaires.

[xli] Parenti, M. (2011). Democracy for the Few (th ed.). Wadsworth.

[xlii] Institute on Taxation and Economic Policy (ITEP). (2025, May 27). House bill giveaway to multinational corporations puts America last. https://itep.org/house-bill-giveaway-to-multinational-corporations-puts-america-last/

[xliii] Institute on Taxation and Economic Policy (ITEP). (2025, May 27). House bill giveaway to multinational corporations puts America last. https://itep.org/house-bill-giveaway-to-multinational-corporations-puts-america-last/

[xliv] Forbes. (2020). The Forbes 400 Self-Made Score. https://www.forbes.com/self-made

[xlv] Business Insider. (2024, February 15). Elon Musk's father owned an emerald mine in apartheid-era Africa. https://www.businessinsider.com/elon-musk-apartheid-emerald-mine-father-2024-2

[xlvi] CNBC. (2024, March 22). Elon Musk's early career: From Zip2 to PayPal. https://www.cnbc.com/elon-musk-early-career-zip2-paypal

[xlvii] Good Jobs First. (2025, February 28). Elon Musk's business empire is built on $38 billion in government funding. https://goodjobsfirst.org/elon-musks-business-empire

[xlviii] ProPublica. (2021, June 8). The Secret IRS Files: How the Wealthiest Avoid Income Tax. https://www.propublica.org/article/secret-irs-files-tax-avoidance

[xlix] Federal Reserve. (2023). Survey of Consumer Finances. https://www.federalreserve.gov/econres/scfindex.htm
[l] Congressional Joint Committee on Taxation. (2024). Estimates of Federal Tax Expenditures. https://www.jct.gov/publications/2024/federal-tax-expenditures
[li] National Employment Law Project. (2022). Warehousing pain: Amazon worker injury rate skyrockets with rapid expansion. https://www.nelp.org/insights-research/warehousing-pain-amazon-worker-injury-rate-skyrockets-with-companys-rapid-expansion-in-new-york-state/
[lii] National Employment Law Project. (2021). Injuries and racial inequity in Amazon's Minnesota operations. https://www.nelp.org/insights-research/injuries-dead-end-jobs-and-racial-inequity-in-amazons-minnesota-operations/
[liii] Seattle Times. (2021). Amazon's workforce split sharply along race and gender lines. https://www.seattletimes.com/business/amazon/amazons-workforce-split-sharply-along-the-lines-of-race-gender-and-pay-new-data-indicates/
[liv] Prison Legal News. (2024). AT&T exploits prison labor. https://www.prisonlegalnews.org/news/1993/apr/15/att-exploits-prison-labor/
[lv] Jacobin. (2024). Wall Street milks the prison system. https://jacobin.com/2024/02/prison-phone-calls-telecom-revenue
[lvi] University of San Francisco. (2015). Incentives to incarcerate: Corporation involvement in prison labor. https://repository.usfca.edu/cgi/viewcontent.cgi?article=1274&context=capstone
[lvii] Supermarket News. (2024). Walmart's pandemic workforce gap for women. https://www.supermarketnews.com/foodservice-

retail/walmart-finds-pandemic-workforce-gap-for-women

[lviii] Vice. (2024). Amazon's gender pay gap secrecy. https://www.vice.com/en/article/nobody-knows-if-amazon-pays-men-more-than-women-but-that-might-change/

[lix] Reddit. (2022, November 14). Jeff Bezos awards Dolly Parton $100 million to give to whatever... Retrieved from https://www.reddit.com/r/Music/comments/yujoxi/jeff_bezos_awards_dolly_parton_100_million_to/

[lx] Counterpunch. (2021, December 1). Tax consequences of Bezos donating $100 million and Musk selling stock worth $5 billion. Retrieved from https://www.counterpunch.org/2021/12/01/tax-consequences-of-bezos-donating-100-million-and-musk-selling-stock-worth-5-billion/

[lxi] Vox. (2019, July 3). Mark Zuckerberg and Cory Booker remade Newark schools. Retrieved from https://www.vox.com/future-perfect/2019/7/3/18629810/mark-zuckerberg-cory-booker-newark-schools

[lxii] EdWeek. (2015, September 9). $100 million, Mark Zuckerberg, and a controversial education experiment. Retrieved from https://www.edweek.org/leadership/opinion-100-million-mark-zuckerberg-and-a-controversial-education-experiment/2015/09

[lxiii] US News Deserts. (n.d.). News deserts and ghost newspapers: Will local news survive? Retrieved from https://www.usnewsdeserts.com/reports/news-deserts-and-ghost-newspapers-will-local-news-survive/the-news-landscape-of-the-future-transformed-and-renewed/technological-capabilities-the-algorithm-as-editor/

[lxiv] Centre for Public Impact. (2025, March 11). The Rockefeller Foundation and philanthropy for social change. Retrieved from

https://centreforpublicimpact.org/public-impact-fundamentals/the-rockefeller-foundation-and-philanthropy-for-social-change/

[lxv] Philanthropy Roundtable. (2023, May 16). The Rockefeller legacy. Retrieved from https://www.philanthropyroundtable.org/magazine/the-rockefeller-legacy/

[lxvi] Econlib. (2018, May 1). A short paragraph full of errors. Retrieved from https://www.econlib.org/archives/2018/05/a_short_paragra.html

[lxvii] Aviation A2Z. (2025, June 3). Countries with highest millionaires and billionaires in the world in 2025. https://aviationa2z.com/index.php/2025/06/03/countries-with-highest-millionaires-and-billionaires-in-the-world-in-2025/

[lxviii] Inequality.org. (2024, September 17). Billionaire wealth keeps growing. https://inequality.org/article/billionaire-wealth-keeps-growing/

[lxix] LSE Blogs. (2025, January 2). Ten facts about wealth inequality in the USA. https://blogs.lse.ac.uk/inequalities/2025/01/02/ten-facts-about-wealth-inequality-in-the-usa/

[lxx] CNBC. (2025, March 6). Wealth creation is booming as U.S. multimillionaire population jumps. https://www.cnbc.com/2025/03/06/wealth-creation-is-booming-as-us-multimillionaire-population-jumps.html

[lxxi] projects.wealth_inequality. (2025-06-08). Writing a book on wealth inequality, focusing on tax policies and government subsidies for billionaires.

[lxxii] Henley & Partners. (2025, May 20). USA Wealth Report 2025. https://www.henleyglobal.com/newsroom/press-releases/usa-wealth-report-2025

[lxxiii] projects.tax_policy_reform. (2025-06-08). Writing a book on IRS reform, focusing on tax evasion by big corporations and churches.

[lxxiv] Inequality.org. (2025, April 1). 2025 is shaping up to be a banner year for global oligarchs. https://inequality.org/article/2025-is-shaping-up-to-be-a-banner-year-for-global-oligarchs/

www.ingramcontent.com/pod-product-compliance
Lightning Source LLC
LaVergne TN
LVHW052245070526
838201LV00113B/348/J